Shapes around the world

By Sarah McPherson

Copyright © Tarva Publishing
www.tarvapublishing.com.au

Cover Illustrations - Lucia Benito

All rights reserved. No part of this book may be reproduced or used in any manner without written permission of the copyright owner except for the use of quotations in a book review.

ISBN: 978-0-6456158-8-3

This is a work of fiction, names, characters, places, and incidents that either are the product of the author's imagination or used factiously. Any resemblances to actual persons, living or dead, events, or locales is entirely coincidental.

To Ashleigh, Madi, Will, Mabel, Ella, Helena and Romeo

You bring so much joy to my life. Thanks for making me an Auntie.

As I travel around the world,

I see shapes everywhere.

But the words are all so different,

Like Il Quadrato in Italian for square

With so many languages to hear,

I have chosen just a few.

So time to learn some shapes,

In a language that is new.

So lets turn the page together,

I have some words to share.

It's time to get started,

with a word like Square.

Square

Italian
Il quadrato

French
carré

Brazilian Portuguese
Quadrado

Spanish
Cuadrado

German
Quadrat

Rectangle

Italian
il rettangolo

French
Le Rectangle

Brazilian Portuguese
retângulo

Spanish
rectángulo

German
Rechteck

Circle

Italian
il cerchio

French
cercle

Brazilian Portuguese
Circulo

Spanish
Circulo

German
Kreis

Triangle

Italian
triangolo

French
Triangle

Brazilian Portuguese
triángulo

Spanish
triángulo

German
Dreick

Diamond

Italian
diamante

French
Diamant

Brazilian Portuguese
Losango

Spanish
El Rombo

German
Raute

Heart

Italian
cuore

French
Coeur

Brazilian Portuguese
coração

Spanish
El corazón

German
Herz

Star

Italian
Stella

French
étoile

Brazilian Portuguese
Estrela

Spanish
La Estella

German
Stern

octagon

Italian
L'Ottagonox

French
Octogone

Brazilian Portuguese
octágono

Spanish
octágono

German
Achteck

Shape

Italian
Forma

French
Forme

Brazilian Portuguese
Forma

Spanish
Forma

German
Form

So did you learn some shapes,

In a language that was new.

In French, Italian, Portuguese,

Spanish and German too.

I hope you had fun,

As you read through the book.

So head back to the start,

To take another look.

Square, Rectangle, Circle, Triangle, Diamond, Heart, Star, Octagon, Shape.

Il quadrato, il rettangolo, il cerchio, Triangolo, Diamante, Cuore, Stella, L'Ottagono, Forma.

carré, Le Rectangle, cercle, Triangle, Diamant, Coeur, étoile, Octogone, Forme.

Quadrado, rectângulo, Círculo, Triângulo, Losango, Coração, Estrela, octágono, Forma.

Cuadrado, rectángulo, Círculo, Triángulo, El Rombo, El corazón, La Estella, octágono, Forma.

Quadrat, Rechteck, Kreis, Dreick, Raute, Herz, Stern, Achteck, Form.

www.ingramcontent.com/pod-product-compliance
Lightning Source LLC
Chambersburg PA
CBHW061808290426
44109CB00031B/2969